CU00821345

ICONIC
MODERN ARCHITECTURE

Douglas Smith

paintings ▪ sketches ▪ journeys

ICONIC
MODERN ARCHITECTURE

Douglas Smith
paintings ▪ sketches ▪ journeys

The exploits of an architect and artist with sketchbook and camera.
Unexpected encounters, surprising connections and stories.

Other books by the same author

LEICESTER Paintings and sketches .... ISBN 9780953812455

LEICESTER, LEICESTERSHIRE RUTLAND

Paintings and sketches .... ISBN 9780953812448

TUSCANY Paintings and sketches .... ISBN 9780953812431

FRANCE Paintings and sketches .... ISBN 9780953812417

LEICESTER Paintings and sketches .... ISBN 9780953812424

ARCHITECTURE INTERIOR LANDSCAPE .... ISBN 9780953812400

HOTEL RESTAURANT DESIGN .... ISBN 0-435-86501-3

Acknowledgements

I would like to thank Christopher Bent, chairman of Leicester Society of Artists who suggested and encouraged me to publish Iconic Modern Architecture to include the exploits with a London Taxi on the Grand Tour. To Edward Moody for the graphic design and to Cliff Watts for scanning the paintings and drawings with great skill.
I am indebted to Kate Ruse for typing and help with Christopher Bent on the text. To Hillary Smith, Shirley Smith and Veronica Rawson for their editing skills, who have put me right when I have got it wrong.
I am pleased to acknowledge the following sources for the quotations.
Albert Einstein, Le Corbusier, Clive James, James Joyce, Frank Lloyd Wright, Norman Foster, Ken Done, Jørn Utzon, Walter Gropius, Mies van der Rohe, Daniel Libeskind, Philip Johnson, Philip Jodidio, James Stirling, Frank Gehry, Richard Rogers, Renzo Piano and Zaha Hadid.

Iconic Modern Architecture

Douglas Smith paintings sketches and journeys

Published in the United Kingdom 2015
Douglas Smith Stimson Partnership Limited
53 Spencefield Lane,
Leicester. LE5 6HH

Printed and bound in the United Kingdom by Greenshires Group Limited

ISBN 9780953812462

Contents

Preface

As both an architect and an artist, an irresistible urge to travel with a sketchbook and camera has been with me for as long as I can remember.

This book is not a history or a travel log but rather it sets out to capture with paintings and sketches some of the exploits I've had over the years in search of many of the new and iconic buildings and gardens of the 20th century. In my youth, travel became feasible with the advent of cheap fares by air, road and rail, and the availability of Youth Hostels across the world. As the century progressed the travel industry began to offer a wider range of special packages, first in Europe and then further afield, enabling more 'technical' visits to be made to areas of interest. I have been privileged to visit Europe, Scandinavia, Canada, America, Japan, South America, Australia, Russia, Africa and China.

The advance in photography, the internet and the digital world has been a great asset. For example when my book *Tuscany Paintings and Sketches* was published in 2009, the University of Leicester Press Office issued an eye-catching press release referring to it with the quote, *transported by brush strokes*. It immediately attracted the attention of the BBC and pages of the book were placed on their website.

So how did this new book come about? We spent Christmas 2014 on the Water in Venice on 'M S Michelangelo', where a number of the guests were recalling when they first visited Venice. To their surprise, I came in 1951 with five students in a 1934 Austin Taxi as part of our 'Grande Tour', but more of this later. On our return home with this story, many friends encouraged me to publish a book of paintings, sketches and stories of my selection of landmark modern buildings and gardens from around the world. What better place to start than in Italy.

San Giorgio Maggiore by Andrea Palladio 1559-80.

Library, Campanile, Doge's Palace

Ca' d'Oro

M.S. Michelangelo with
Santa Maria della Salute

Caffè Florian

My aims are twofold. Firstly to engender in all who read the book a love and enthusiasm for good modern architecture and gardens. Secondly to continue to raise money and promote the work of the 'Hope Foundation for Cancer Research'. When you buy this book, you will be getting a unique insight into the architecture of the world, and also helping in a real way in the fight against cancer in Leicestershire and Rutland.

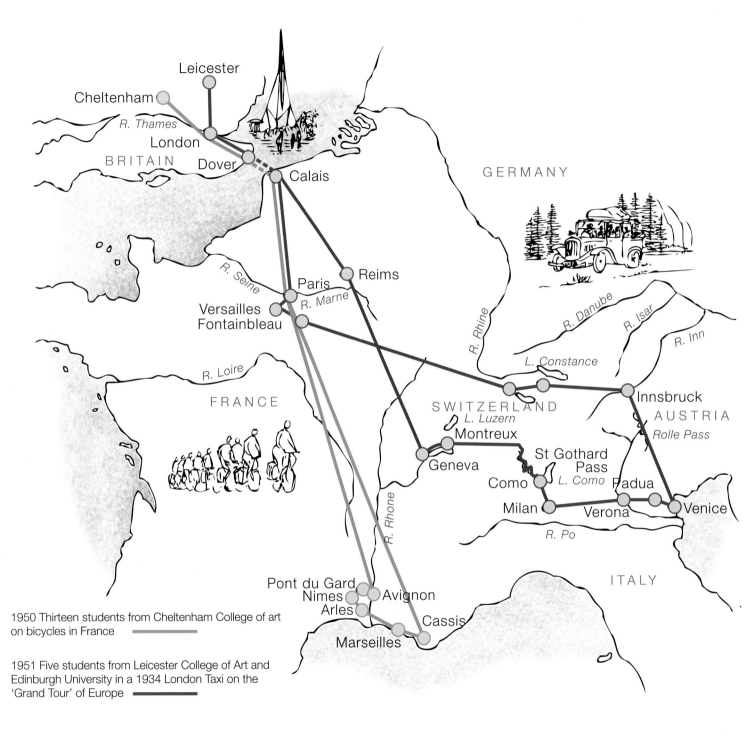

Leicester

Cheltenham

R. Thames

London

BRITAIN

Dover

Calais

GERMANY

R. Seine

Reims

Paris

R. Marne

Versailles
Fontainbleau

R. Loire

FRANCE

R. Rhine

R. Danube

R. Isar

R. Inn

L. Constance

SWITZERLAND

Innsbruck

AUSTRIA

L. Luzern

Rolle Pass

Montreux

St Gothard
Pass

Geneva

R. Rhone

Como

L. Como

Padua

Milan

Verona

Venice

R. Po

ITALY

Pont du Gard
Nimes

Avignon

Arles

Cassis

1950 Thirteen students from Cheltenham College of art
on bicycles in France

Marseilles

1951 Five students from Leicester College of Art and
Edinburgh University in a 1934 London Taxi on the
'Grand Tour' of Europe

Introduction

Architecture is that great living creative spirit which from generation to generation, from age to age, proceeds, persists, creates, according to the nature of man, and his circumstances as they change. That is really architecture.
  Frank Lloyd Wright.

I was born in Kendal and moved to Evesham at the age of four, where, as a child, I was always drawing and making things in wood. At sixteen I went to Cheltenham College of Art where the enlightened Principal encouraged me to join the painting, sculpture, and pottery classes – essentially an early version of an art foundation course. This eventually led me to concentrate on architecture as I was inspired by the buildings and writing of Frank Lloyd Wright.

The search for inspirational modern architecture started in my early days as a student with two incredible journeys and a memorable exhibition.
It was first on bicycles in France.
The second was in an old London taxi in Europe.
The exhibition was the 1951 Festival of Britain in London.
Later the search was to spread across the world.

France and the buildings of Le Corbusier, on bicycles.

In 1950 on completion of our Diploma Course, the equivalent of a first degree nowadays, we wanted to see some great modern architecture. I had met an Italian girl who had come to a Boarding School in England the year the Second World War started and could not return home. At the end of the war she decided to stay and came to Cheltenham where we met. With her language skills and a shared enthusiasm for travel and architecture we organised a group of colleagues to join us to see in three-dimensional form some of the outstanding modern buildings we had studied. Despite having little money, France appeared a possibility and so we set about planning for a group of thirteen students to travel on bicycles and long distances on trains in search of the work of Le Corbusier. We found cheap accommodation at the Cité Universitaire in Paris and other youth hostels in the various locations for the trip.

The group on the ferry

Pavillon Suisse west front

East front

Pavillon Suisse, Cité Universitaire

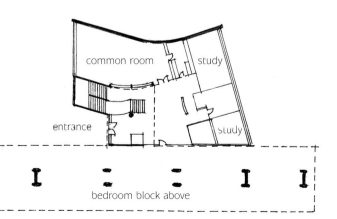

Mural by Le Corbusier

Ville Savoy

Le Corbusier, an important architect of the first half of the 20th century and the founder of 'modern architecture', attracted us through his work and writing. We started at the Maison Suisse, the student hostel at the Cité Universitaire Paris and we were not disappointed. It was built in 1930-2 and comprised of three distinct elements expressed clearly. A rectangular box was poised on concrete pilotis for the study bedrooms, whilst the adjacent staircase and toilet could be found in the curved rectangular vertical block. At ground level a single storey communal entrance led to the lounge/common room. This became the model for 'halls of residence' around the world.

Bicycles were a good way to explore Paris and the surroundings. We negotiated and traversed the Place de la Concorde like a centipede and survived! At that time there was no circulatory traffic system. We were surprised to find Villa Savoy at Poissy, a beautiful unique house of great architectural quality. Neglected by its farmer owner, it stood in a field of rough grass.

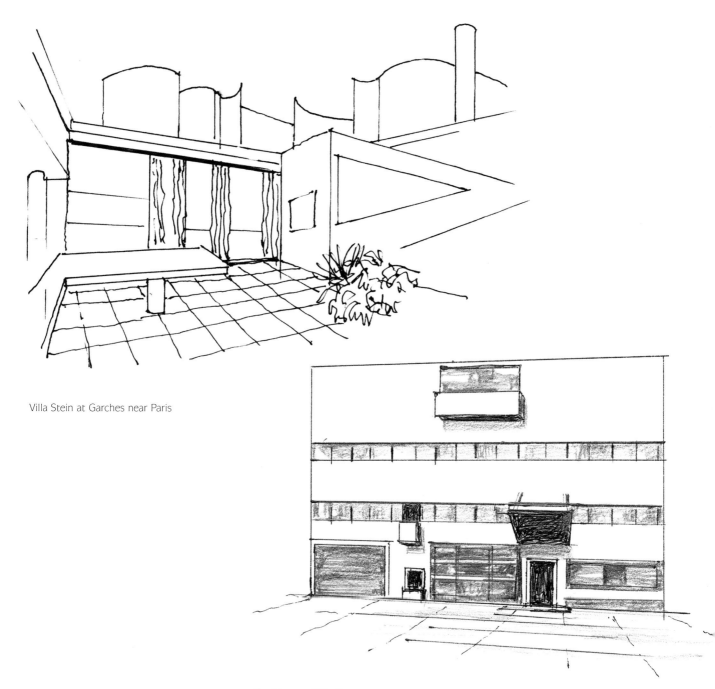

Villa Stein at Garches near Paris

Roof terrace Villa Savoy

Pont Saint-Bénezet Avignon

A few days later we put our bicycles on the train to Avignon where we found the Youth Hostel with a stunning view of Pont St-Bénézet and the Palais des Papes. It took several days to cycle to Nimes to see the Pont du Gard and Maison Carrée, both built by the Romans. Then to Arles, followed by a long ride to see the flats of Unité d'Habitation in Marseilles, which was to show to the world Le Corbusier's concept of the modern city 'La Ville Radieuse'.

The design made full use of his 'modular' system of proportions based on a mathematical progression. The 'Unite' is virtually the Maison Suisse multiplied by ten. It was a building for a whole

Pont du Gard AD 150
Highest bridge for 500 years at 48 m

Unité d'Habitation, Marseilles in 1951
completed in 1953.

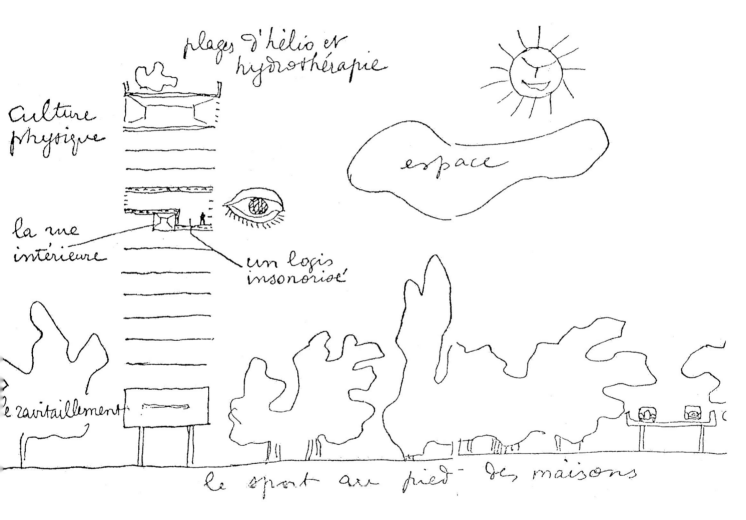

plages d'hélio et
hydrothérapie

Culture
physique

la rue
intérieure

un logis
insonorisé

espace

le ravitaillement

le sport au pied des maisons

Diagrammatic section by Le Corbusier

19

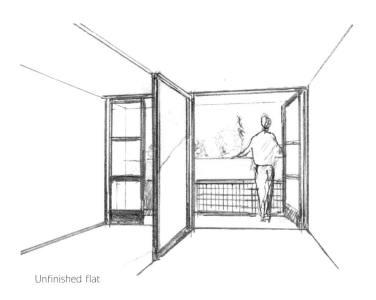

Unfinished flat

Unité d'Habitation, west front

Roofscape with recreation facilities

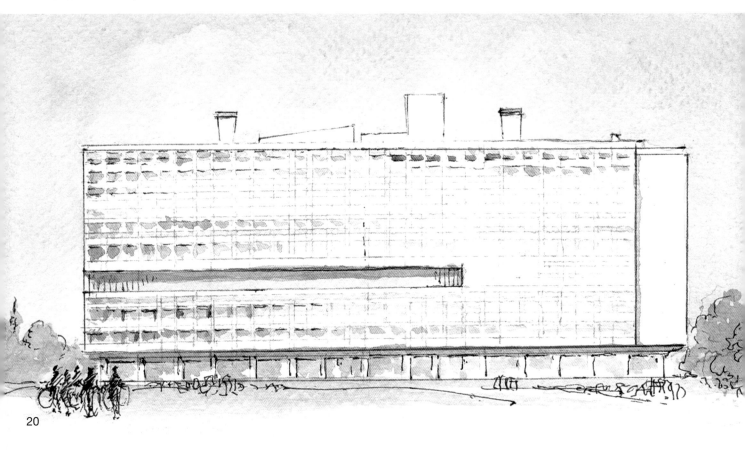

community with 350 single and two storey flats, a shopping area and recreation facilities in a park landscape. The construction work was finished when we saw it but it would be two years before final completion. The fitting out and experimentation with different coloured panels was still in progress. We were delighted to find there were no barriers to visiting or climbing to roof level. 'Health and Safety' was yet to be invented.

Having had our fill of architecture, we placed our bikes on the roof of the local bus to reach the Youth Hostel at Cassis on the mountain to the east of Marseilles, only to find the beds we had booked were not available. The terrace was a little hard but it was a warm night and we enjoyed using our sleeping bags, with the stars making a wonderful ceiling. We returned the next day by train through Paris to London as very happy students. Mission successfully accomplished.

To complete my studies I came to Leicester School of Architecture and my Italian friend went to Edinburgh University.

Last day at the Youth Hostel at Cassis

A Grand Tour with a London Taxi 1951

In Leicester, at the College of Art and Technology, I shared a study bedroom in the hall of residence with a textile student. My enthusiasm for the successful French visits sparked an interest that led to a brilliant idea for a trip to Europe. We found it was possible to buy a 1934 London Taxi for £125.00. We were keen to go and attempt this adventure. Including my friend from Edinburgh, we only needed to find two more students to reduce the cost to £25.00 a head, and we could begin the adventure.

After much discussion we planned a visit to include France, Switzerland, Italy, Austria and Germany. The father of my friend, the textile student, negotiated a good deal for the purchase of the Taxi and all was set for the summer of 1951.

On the agenda and of special interest for the architects, was to see some of the fine new architecture and engineering projects, particularly the elegant bridges designed by Robert Maillart.

In the Spring we took delivery of the Taxi and practiced our driving and double de-clutching, which was needed for gear changing with the crash gearbox of the vehicle.

At the end of term we met in London to begin the drive to Dover. The tents were stowed on the roof of the vehicle. At Dover the car was lifted by crane onto the ferry. There was no drive on and off facility at this time.

Driving across northern France we made use of the tents before we got to Lake Geneva. One of the group had stayed many times with his parents in a hotel at Montreux. He volunteered to find out if they had any cheap accommodation. He found that there was a vacant staff flat that we could have, providing we didn't go into the hotel. We were able to make use of the kitchen facilities resulting in a very inexpensive stay. My Italian friend went on to Milan by train where we were to meet a few days later.

Bridge by Engineer Robert Mailart

First camp

Venice Santa Maria della Salute

We decided to christen the Taxi 'Gussie' and from now on I will refer to it by that name. The first test was to be the St Gotthard Pass on our journey to Italy. At the bottom of the Pass we were having coffee when an expensive British car drove by but did not acknowledge our friendly wave. As we set out again we realized that it was going to be a difficult task and we would need to stop frequently to prevent the engine overheating. At the top of the Pass, having taken advantage of these frequent stops, we passed the luxury British car with its engine boiling over and we waved goodbye to its occupants as we continued our journey to Milan.

My friend's parents gave us accommodation, allowing us to sleep in the sitting room of their large house in Milan, before we decided to move on to Verona, Vicenza, Padua and Venice. On the journey we made one stop and fortunately found a friendly farmer who allowed us to use his barn as it was too wet for the tents.

Grand Canal from Accademia Bridge

Venice was a new experience, a magical city with canals not roads. We soon realized it was exerting the same effect on us as it did on Byron, Shelley Henry James and many others. It was a treat to discover the newly opened Guggenheim Museum and the works of Brancusi 'Bird in Space' bought direct by Peggy Guggenheim. The 'Arc of Petals' by Alexander Calder remains in the memory. It was a privilege to have a friend who spoke the language and negotiated a cheap rate to explore the smaller canals by gondola.

The next challenge for 'Gussie' was the Rolle Pass as we travelled north to the beautiful town of Innsbruck in the Tirol where we were excited to see a number of people in national costume. We then went to Lake Constance and to Amriswil where we stayed in the family home of two overseas students from the Fashion Department of the Leicester College of Art and Technology. Their parents were wonderful hosts and we enjoyed luxury accommodation and fine food.

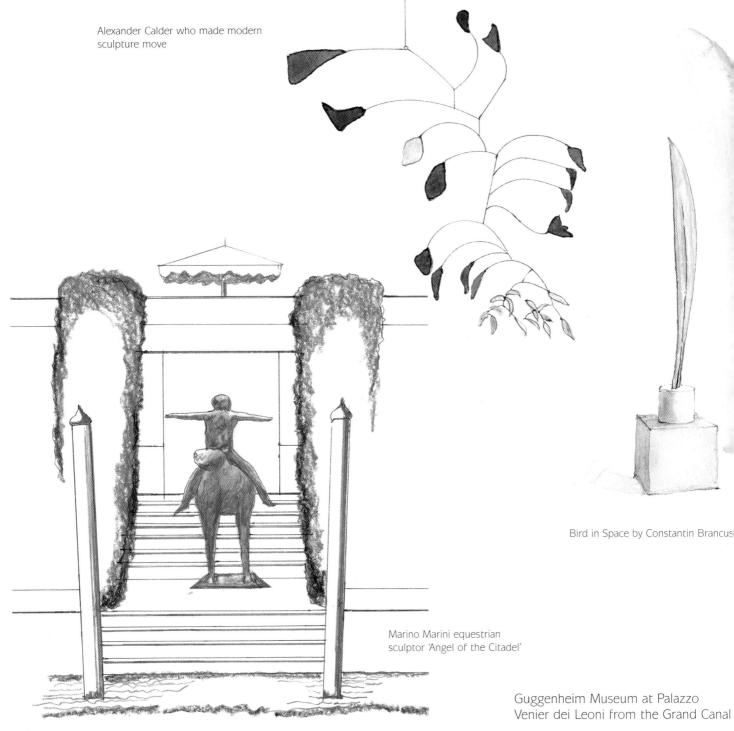

Alexander Calder who made modern sculpture move

Marino Marini equestrian sculptor 'Angel of the Citadel'

Bird in Space by Constantin Brancus

Guggenheim Museum at Palazzo Venier dei Leoni from the Grand Canal

group with us and 'Gussie' on the Rolle Pass

Eiffel Tower 1889 by Gustave Eiffel

We encountered our next problem in Zurich where Gussie's fan belt broke. We were informed by the garage mechanic that the type of web belt that was required to fix the problem had long since become unavailable. However this resourceful individual managed to use a modern 'V' belt, making it function by increasing the pressure on the dynamo and the alternator. We got home safely. Returning via France, we stopped to visit the Palace of Fontainebleau. In Paris we had an exciting crossing of the Place de la Concorde. Finally a happy landing as Gussie was hoisted on and off the ferry after a fascinating journey of 2,500 miles.

Crystal Palace. Great Exhibition of 1851

The Crystal Palace was its centrepiece in Hyde Park, London, designed by Joseph Paxton. The 19 acre main hall, which measured 1,848 ft. long by 408 ft wide and 72 ft high was made from a steel frame erected in 17 weeks and was ready for use in 39 weeks. The building was simple and elegant using only two materials, steel and glass.

Festival of Britain 1951

In the autumn of 1950 I joined the fourth year at the School of Architecture, Leicester College of Art. There was a dedicated staff with a head of year who organized a monthly, one-day sketch design, of a large complex building. The first third of the day was spent on research, the second resolving the design and the final third on presentation. We were encouraged to use not only steel and concrete frames but new innovative construction using thin folded slabs and shells made of concrete.

The Festival of Britain gave us an opportunity to see how the younger architects were responding to the brief to promote Britain's contribution to science, technology, industrial design, architecture and art. The country was reminded of the Great Exhibition of 1851, which was a showcase to the world.

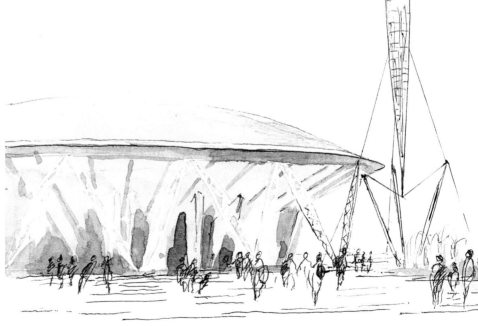

Dome of Discovery Architect Ralph Tubbs

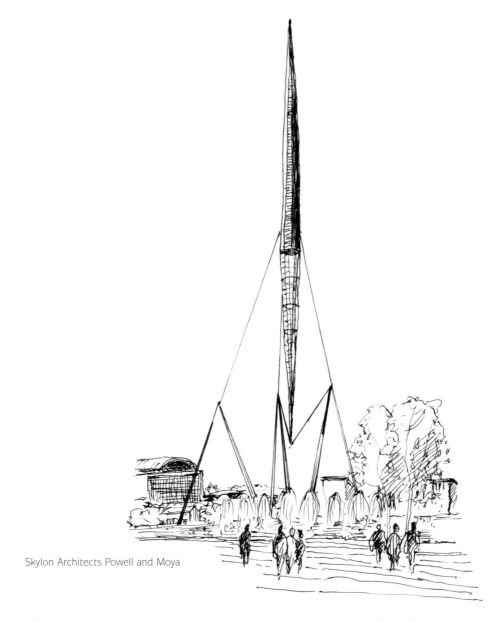

Skylon Architects Powell and Moya

The 1951 Exhibition design group was headed by Hugh Casson with Misha Black, Ralph Tubbs, James Holland and James Gardener. The Exhibition was the climax of four years intense work and it became a landmark in Britain's history. It conveyed a story of optimism after the War and signaled a better future through new architecture, replacing the slums of pre war Britain.

Royal Festival Hall
Architects Leslie Martin, Peter Moro and Robert Mathew of the GLC

The Skylon by Powell and Moya was an exciting structure combining architecture and engineering. It was an abiding symbol. The Dome of Discovery was a 365 ft diameter saucer-shaped roof designed by Ralph Tubbs and engineer Sir Ralph Freeman. It was the largest exhibition space. Imaginative landscaping played a major part in linking the design of the South Bank together. The lasting legacy was the The Royal Festival Hall, designed by Leslie Martin, Peter Moro and Robert Mathew from the Architects' Department of London County Council.

Forest Crematorium by Gunnar Asplund.

Scandinavian design emerged in the 1950s
Denmark, Sweden and Finland
Designs spearheaded by architects in Denmark by Arne Jacobson and Jørn Utzon,
in Sweden by Gunnar Asplund and in Finland by Eero Saarinen and Alvar Aalto

School of Museum Studies University of Leicester
Architects Douglas Smith Stimson Partnership

Denmark, Sweden and Finland 1952 – 2007
Brief Review of DSSP Ltd 1960 – 2000

There were interesting buildings to visit in Scandinavia. First to Denmark and Sweden on bicycles in 1952, then in 1962 by car with our 11 month old blue-eyed, blond haired son, where he was greeted as a little Dane. Later, in 1967, we had a fly drive visit to Finland with our two children. Scandinavian design emerged in the 1950s and the movement was characterized by simplicity, minimalism and function and this was to influence the designs of my practice from 1960 – 2000.

To celebrate graduation in 1952, I, with three other students, decided to visit Denmark and Sweden on bicycles before starting to work. Taking the ferry to Esbjerg, we cycled to the interesting new buildings of Aarhus before travelling to Copenhagen. The University is acknowledged as one of the twelve most meaningful architectural works in Denmark, designed by C. F. Møller Architects. The main buildings are situated on a beautiful hilly landscape. We admired the yellow brick buildings fully integrated with the landscape; a beautiful campus which has received international recognition.

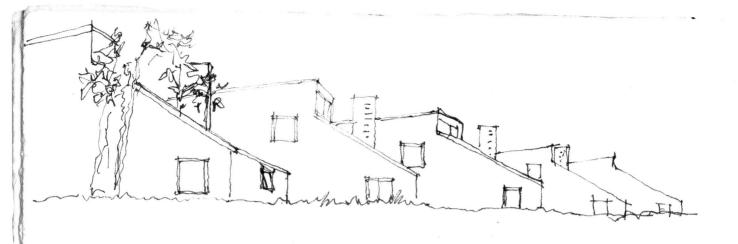

Houses Klampenborg, Copenhagen Architect Arne Jacobsen

Chairs by Arne Jacobsen

Court Houses, Elsinore Architect Jørn Utzon

Aarhus University. Architects C F Møller

Stelling House.
Architect Arne Jacobsen

Copenhagen gave us the opportunity to see the influential work of Arne Jacobsen and Jørn Utzon. Arne Jacobsen considered the building as only part of the design as a setting for life, judging furniture and fittings, floor and wall materials, lighting and window details to be just as important as the building.

A small commercial building Stelling House was a simple design and the first modern building in the old town; not loved at first but soon accepted as a fine example.

In Klampenborg north of Copenhagen we went to see the Søholm chain a semi-detached housing development. The houses, built of yellow brick with roofs in dark asbestos cement slates, were designed to preserve the large trees on the site. All houses had views over the picturesque straits separating Denmark and Sweden. One house for the architect, with a beautifully designed garden, also served as a show house and was available to view

Arne Jacobsen's great international commission was St. Catherine's College Oxford in the 1960s.

His chairs became internationally famous throughout the world and are still sold today, manufactured by Fritf Hansen's Eftf. A/S. In 1952 the stacking chair became available for mass production, with the seat and back moulded from a single piece of laminated veneer supported on light tubular steel legs. In 1959 he became known for the 'Egg and Swan' chairs. His skill extended to beautiful simple tableware of stainless steel.

Louisiana Museum of Modern Art 1958 north of Copenhagen
Architects Jorgen Bo & Vilhelm Wohlert

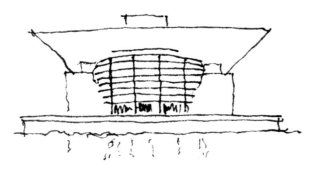

Opera House Architects Henning Larson

Black Diamond Architects Schmidt, Hammer & Larson

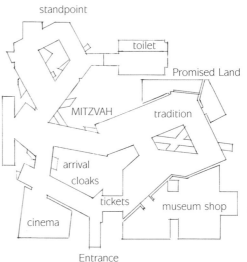

standpoint

toilet

Promised Land

MITZVAH

tradition

arrival

cloaks

tickets

museum shop

cinema

Entrance

LOGO – MITZV

Danish Jewish Muse
Copenhag
Architects Daniel Libesk
Plan inspired by the Jew
concept of MITZVAH '
good de
The four Hebrew letters in
word form the basic p

The impressive Court Houses, Elsinore houses by Jørn Utzon are based on a square plan with living rooms and bedrooms on an L shape plan with the courtyard garden overlooking a shared parkland.

On our second visit to Copenhagen we were impressed with Louisiana Museum, north of the city overlooking the sea, designed by architects Jorgen Bo & Vilhelm Wohlert in 1958. It is a complete composition of building and site, retaining the old house, the roof floats over the landscape and plate glass circulation spaces link the galleries. It is a type of abstract design where plants and building form the setting for enjoying art. There is a beautiful sculpture garden.

From Malmo, Sweden we took the train to Stockholm. From the train we saw the 1929 City Hall by Ragnar Ostberg, an early example of modern architectural design of a civic building.

Stockholm Town Hall 1909-23
Architects Raynar Ostberg

Youth Hostel AF Chapman
(Dunboyne 1888-1915 full-rigged streel ship)

Our stay was on the floating ship, the AF Chapman, formerly the Dunboyne (1888-1915) it is a full-rigged steel ship which has been converted into a youth hostel with 285 beds. A unique treat which we enjoyed.

The stunning Forest Crematorium, Emskede 1934-40 by Gunnar Asplund stands at the top of a gently sloping hill. The cross dominates the simple but dramatic group of buildings linked by a large portico and it was the highlight of our visit to Sweden.

In Helsinki, Finland we were in search of the work of Eero Saarinen, Alvar Aalto and Marimekko fabrics. To walk round buildings so familiar from photographs is a treat. I remembered the design of

Marimekko fabrics with passion for
bright colours and patterns. Unmissable
bold black-and-white designs.

Saarinen from TWA Terminal Kennedy Airport New York designed in 1962 and was pleased to see his earlier designed Railway Station in Helsinki.

There are too many buildings to list but the following remain in my memory. The Tuberculous Sanatorium, Paimio in reinforced concrete, rendered and painted white was so simple and beautiful and was one of Aalto's early buildings. The Town Hall, Säynätsalo 1952 is impressive and fascinating with the timber exposed trusses of the council chamber.

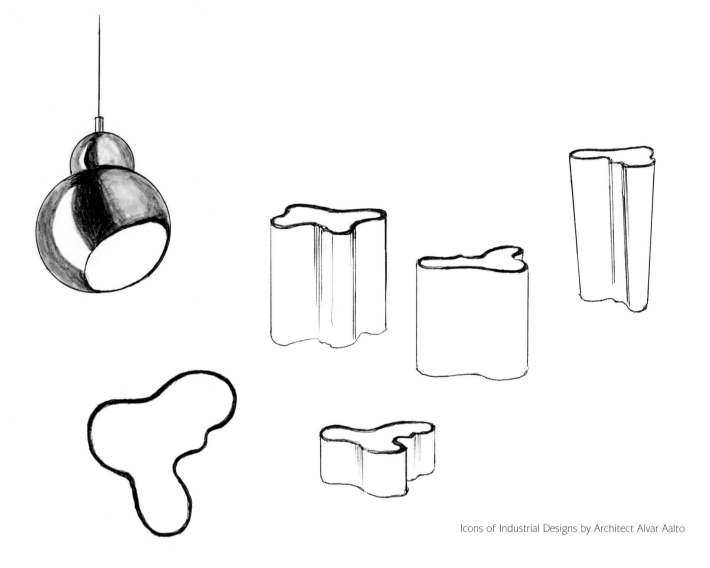

Icons of Industrial Designs by Architect Alvar Aalto

The son of Armi Marimekko with his wife came to De Montfort University in Leicester and we became friends. Before they returned to Helsinki we were invited to make contact if we came to Finland. In due course we did, and Risto collected us from our hotel, taking us to his parents' summer house where we were invited to a party being held there. The children were warmly invited too and we arrived to discover the 'summer house' consisted of three large farms around a lake. After settling in, we enjoyed a sauna, where there were 50 towels in the changing room – one for each guest.

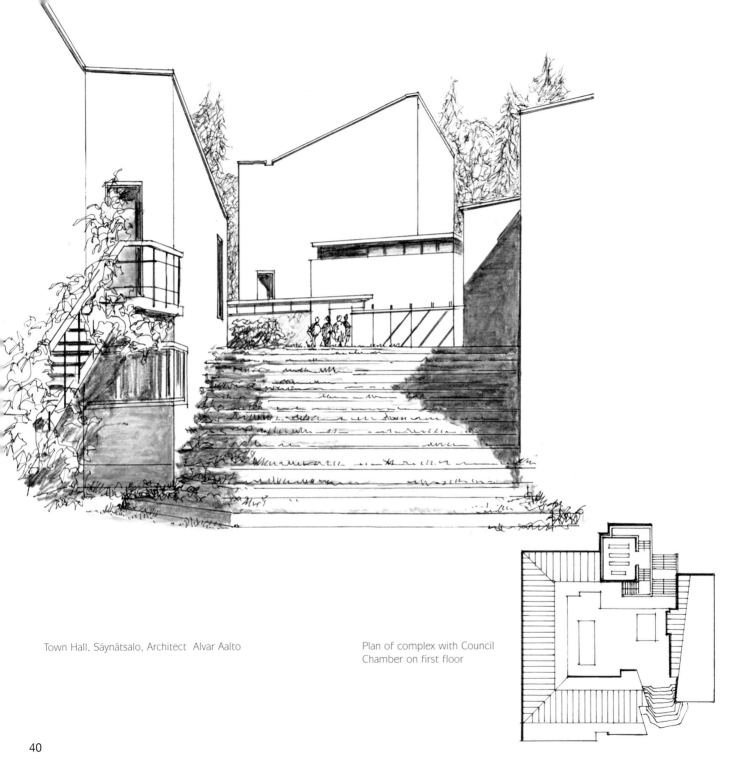

Town Hall, Säynätsalo, Architect Alvar Aalto

Plan of complex with Council Chamber on first floor

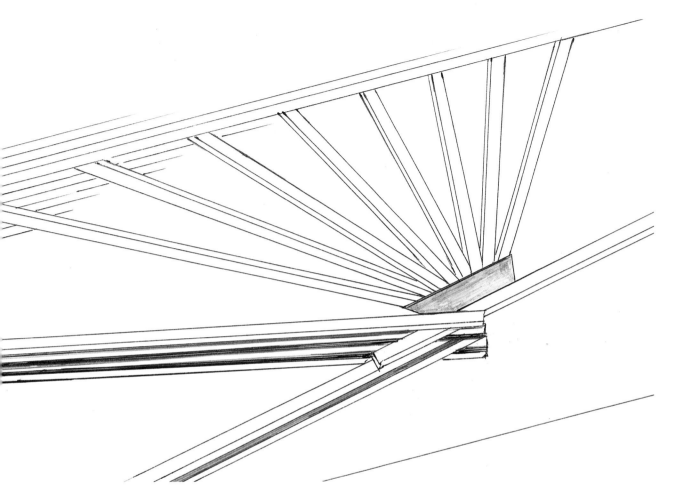

Interesting roof truss to the Council Chamber, Alvar Aalto

That evening we sat down in an open barn to crayfish, vodka and wine; with so little meat on a crayfish it was good we did not have to drive. Big candles in large glass vases lit up the complex. The next day we visited the factory of Marimekko to see their graphic designs for the textiles and the large screen printing in progress. It was clear to see why the bold fabrics and bright, simple designs strongly influenced late 20th century taste.

Looking back and trying to be objective in briefly reviewing the work of DSSP Ltd the commissions were of a similar scale to the buildings we visited in Scandinavia and similar use of materials; we also

The focal centre was the main auditorium
with an outdoor theatre inspired by the
amphitheatre of Delphi, Greece.

Institute of Technology Otaniemi, Architects Alvar Aalto

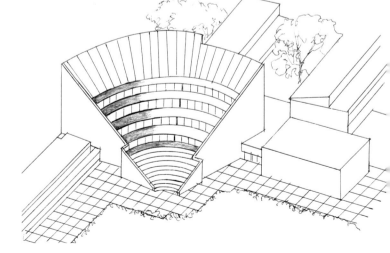

Timber ceiling

Bent wood furniture by Alvar Aalto

made where ever possible the design of the buildings complete with interior and landscape. It was established in 1960 as a multi-disciplined team of Architects, Landscape Architects and Interior Designers. The Practice philosophy was to produce the best possible design for each project without preconceived ideas.

The following are a few examples from the 3176 projects.

For the University of Leicester, a small Sports Pavilion (demolished) for a larger one; School of Museums Studies, Professorial housings complete with a powerful landscape design and the Chaplaincy Centre.

Spec builders Court Yard Houses, Landscape Drive Housing and many developments for Leicester Housing Association.

Resources Centre for the Blind.

United States of America Pavilion
Architect Buckminster Fuller

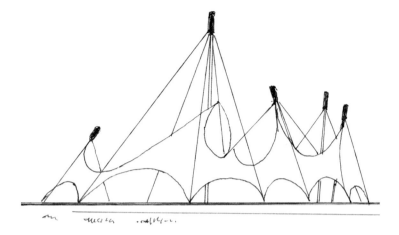

West German Pavilion scheme drawing

Expo 67 Montreal Canada and America 1967

The Architectural Press was giving publicity to the new architecture to be seen in Montreal by leading architects involved in the National Pavilions. This was also the Centennial celebration year for Canada. The motto that the country had adopted for the event was, in the words of Albert Schweitzer, 'set a good example for the world. If you are excellent, if you are high quality, the world will imitate you'. I had remained a friend of the student who joined the School of Architecture with me and had graduated at the same time in 1952. We discussed Expo 67 and decided that this would be an opportunity we should not miss, and made arrangements to travel to Canada and the United States of America. There was a further reason to go. I had set up in practice in Leicester in 1960 and had been appointed by the University of Leicester to design a small sports pavilion in 1963. This appointment led to a commission to design the School of Education, comprising the conversion of three Victorian buildings and a free-standing large library. Around this time the University of Yale had commissioned Gordon Bunshaft of Skidmore, Owings and Merrill to design the Beinecke Rare Book Library at the University. The Bursar at the University of Leicester offered to make an appointment for me to see the building.

West German Pavilion Architect Frei Otto

The city of Montreal embraced Expo 67 with enthusiasm and this was reflected in one of the best exhibitions I have seen. Three Pavilions stand out in my memory. The Pavilion of the United States of America designed by Buckminster Fuller was one of the most popular with over five million visitors. The building was distinguished by its large twenty-storey geodesic dome with an acrylic skin. The site's Minirail was a distinctive feature of Expo and it attracted the public's interest as they passed through the building.

The West German Pavilion was designed by Frei Otto, a German architect and structural engineer. His wonderful use of lightweight tensile membrane structures resulted in a beautiful building but this failed to make a lasting impact on visitors as they passed though the pavilion as it lacked an attention-grabbing exhibition.

British Pavilion Architect Basil Spence

The British Pavilion designed by Basil Spence was perceived by many to be the most popular and received over 5 million visitors. It featured a fascinating exhibition tracing the history of Britain's inventions and contribution to science. A sculpture by Henry Moore was located in a pool outside the Pavilion. It was interesting and sad for an architect to find that it is not necessarily the best architecture but the building's contents that makes the biggest impact on the public.

Habitat 67 Architects Moshe Safdie

In addition Montreal had engaged Moshe Safdie, a young Israeli Canadian architect to design a unique social housing complex as 'city within a city,' Habitat 67 and this was the highlight of our visit. This was a group of houses comprising 354 identical pre-fabricated concrete forms arranged in various combinations and reaching up to 12 storeys in height. Together these units created 146 residences of varying size and configuration, each formed from one to eight linked concrete units. The complex originally contained 158 apartments, but several apartments have since been joined to create larger units therefore reducing the total number. Each unit is connected to at least one private terrace, which can range from approximately 225 to 1,000 square feet in size. This was a piece of brilliant design, and so popular that it is now luxury flats and not social housing.

Rare Book Library, Yale University Architect Gordon Bunshaft of SOM

It was time to move on and we had booked the night Greyhound coach to New York giving us a four-hour stop over at Yale University. Traveling by coach in 1967 without the facility of coffee bar stops, made us feel we were second-class citizens. We arrived at Yale at 7.00am with nothing to do so we decided to see what was happening at the University. When we arrived the janitors welcomed us and when they discovered that we wanted to see the Rare Book Library they offered to take us there. We had a very thorough examination of the building, both inside and out. The Library was unique insofar that the external walls were of very thin marble to reduce the light coming into the rare book space. This gave a subtle impact to the interior.

From the 'Top of the Rock' looking towards Central
Park, lake and Metropolitan Museum of Art
projecting into the Park landscape.

Kandinsky

Frank Lloyd Wright
.......*It was to make the building and the paintings an uninterrupted, beautiful symphony such as never existed in the World of Art before*

View from the top floor of the great central space with a single continuous ramp to the ground floor.

Logo

Guggenheim Museum

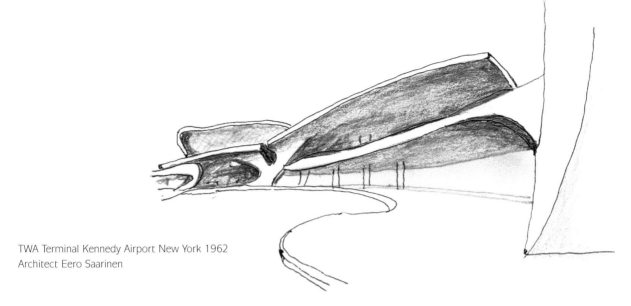

TWA Terminal Kennedy Airport New York 1962
Architect Eero Saarinen

At 9.00am when we met the Director, he informed us that he had a full programme for the day. We said that we were sorry but we had to rejoin our coach at 11.00am to continue our journey to New York. I told him that I would like some photographs of the building. All the arrangements were pulled forward and they managed to cram the whole day's programme into a two-hour slot enabling us to rejoin our coach for the onward journey. How the Americans look after their guests!

To get a taste of New York in three days was an impossible task and we had to be extremely selective. We were impressed to see the skyscrapers packed closely together. We made time to see the view from the top of the Empire State Building. From our lofty vantage point we were able to pick out the distinctive Art Deco designed tower of the Chrysler Building and see the compact high density of Manhattan.

Frank Lloyd Wright designed the Guggenheim Museum as a 'total work of art', an organic space. It was an experience. As we entered the building the staff ushered everyone to lifts to the top floor. After admiring the great space we slowly descended the spiral ramp. Should the paintings be hung parallel with the slope or a true horizontal? It was difficult to decide. We stopped to look at the wonderful collection of works by Kandinsky and spent a long time looking both at the paintings and sculptures. It is a fascinating building but a challenge for curators.

It was a pleasant surprise to find the unusual design of the Whitney Museum by Marcel Bruer close by. There was only time to see the exterior of the simple elegant and beautiful Lever Building designed by Gordon Bunshaft of SOM and the Seagram Building by Mies van der Rohe before it was time to return to England.

View from the Empire State Building with the 'Art Deco'
Chrysler Building. Architect William von Alen 1928-30

Powerful statue of a shogun outside the Imperial Palace,
Tokyo

Nijo-jo Castle, Tokyo 1626

'Memoirs of a Geisha'. Screen adaptation of Arthur Golden's novel 1997 was good preparation for the first visit to Japan

Japan 1970 and 2006

In 1967 I was elected to the Council of the Royal Institute of British Architects and soon found I was the youngest member. Outside the Council chamber those who had been to Canada for Expo were still talking about the unique buildings they had seen there.

When it was announced that Expo 70 was to be in Japan, it was not for Expo that we visited but the opportunity to come face to face with the architecture, landscape and culture of Japan. Architects, rather like their Parisian artist predecessors, Monet and Matisse, were being inspired by the Far East. At the beginning of the 20th century architects like Frank Lloyd Wright and others had discovered the outstanding architecture of the Imperial Palaces, temples and landscapes in Kyoto where there was a fusion of buildings with gardens. Gradually a small group of architects from the RIBA decided that a visit was feasible.

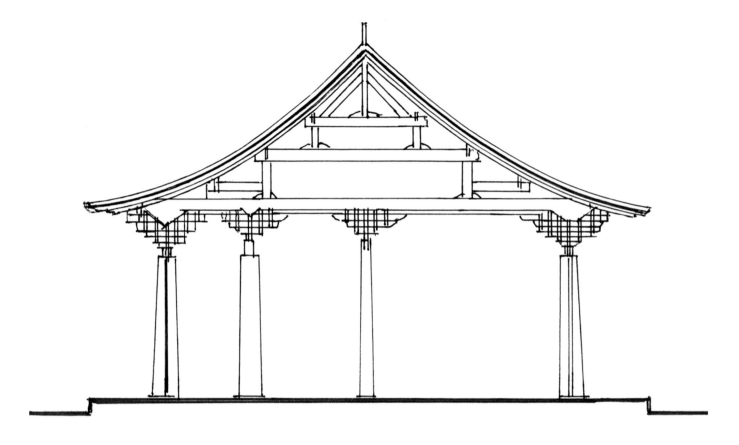

TRADITIONAL JAPAN

Typical section of a Japanese building. The roof structure resolves all the forces to a vertical load onto the columns with no bracing required.

Olympic Gymnasium Tokyo 1961 Architect Kenzo Tange

The visit started in Tokyo and soon we discovered the tour operators had little idea of what was required to satisfy this group of architects. However it was interesting to get a good understanding of the difference between traditional building construction in the east compared with the west. The west developed from post and lintel construction where the walls are a key element in stabilizing the structure like a box. In the east all the structural stress are resolved in the complex roof construction with no stress in the pillars which have only a vertical load to take, like a table. Therefore it was possible for the internal and external spaces to merge in the east where walls could be lightweight screens. This gave the designers an opportunity to create beautiful integrated architecture and landscape.

We struggled to see all the buildings on our list in Tokyo. The next stop was Mount Fuji for one night. On our arrival the fog was so dense that it was impossible to see the mountain. Our guide said that he thought we must have arrived at our destination but other members of the party said we were by a lake and our hotel was supposed to be half way up the mountain. Eventually we arrived and a meeting after dinner was arranged with the guide to agree the program for Kyoto, the next day. We told him that we expected to see the Imperial Palace. He informed us that this was not possible and that we should have organized the visit 12 months before our trip and even then we would not

Mount Fuji in the distance and tea plantations in the foreground

Japanese Camellias

Minimum use of water to maximum effect

JAPANESE GARDENS

necessarily have been granted permission. He then informed us that the temples that we were keen to visit would not open until 10.00am. We asked him why the hotel was so quiet and he told us that it was a honeymooners' hotel! After this very unsatisfactory meeting, he swiftly disappeared. Fortunately one of our party spoke Japanese and he said that he would phone the Imperial Palace on our arrival in Kyoto.

Early next morning there was a lot of noise on Mount Fuji. We went outside and discovered the sun was shining. All the young couples were out taking photographs or being photographed in the magical light of Japan with the incredible mountain as the backdrop. The cherry blossom that we had missed in Tokyo was in full bloom because of the colder air at the different altitude.

In Kyoto I told the group I had arranged an early call and would go to visit two temples, which were not on the guide's list. To my surprise next morning every one was in reception and together we discovered they were working temples and open. The custom on entering Temples is to remove ones shoes. What a difference it makes to visit a building in stocking feet and to squat and look and admire the proportions and beauty of merging landscape with the building.

Mount Fuji & cherry blossom bathed in sunshine

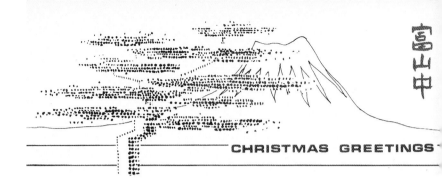

CHRISTMAS GREETINGS

Our friend who spoke Japanese rang the Imperial Palace and informed them that a group of architects from the ROYAL Institute of British Architects would like to have permission to visit the garden and Palace the next day. Permission was granted.

The Katsura Villa was an unforgettable experience. There was no formal approach as we find in the West, like Versailles for example or our English Palaces. The front is laid out as a beautiful garden with stepping stones leading to the entrance to the Villa. The late Bruno Taut, the celebrated German architect, once admired the stone pavement for it being exquisitely laid out from a practical and aesthetic point of view. The villa staff had also arranged a tea ceremony. A new experience, in a calm atmosphere where we squatted on an elevated floor covered with Tatami mats. The tea, more like soup, was served by elegant girls in traditional costumes. It was a magical time as we absorbed the atmosphere with the shimmering light from the lake in the beautiful garden beyond. The half-day visit went too quickly but we did see the whole complex that was beautifully simple with its white outer walls and elevated floors and the roof of timber shingles floating above to complete the picture.

Ryoan-ji with the most famous garden in Japan; a Zen Buddhist temple 1499

Next stop was the Nijo-jo Castle, built in 1603, with its magnificently decorated gate and wooden 'nightingale' floor. It was called this because any footstep would produce a faint, birdlike chirping sound, which would wake the sleeping princess and warn her of impending danger. We then moved on to the wonderful Golden Pavilion at Kankaku-ji, a Buddhist temple set on a lake and later to the exquisite Ryoan-ji Temple and the Zen Garden with the 15 rocks in five groups symbolizing the story of a tigress crossing the river with her cubs. The water is represented by raked sand.

We made a brief visit to Osaka where Expo 70 was held before returning to Britain.

In 2006 we made a second visit to Japan that gave an opportunity to visit Tokyo and Kyoto and confirm my admiration of the beautiful integrated Palaces and Temples with their fascinating landscape gardens.

Katsura Imperial Villa, Kyoto

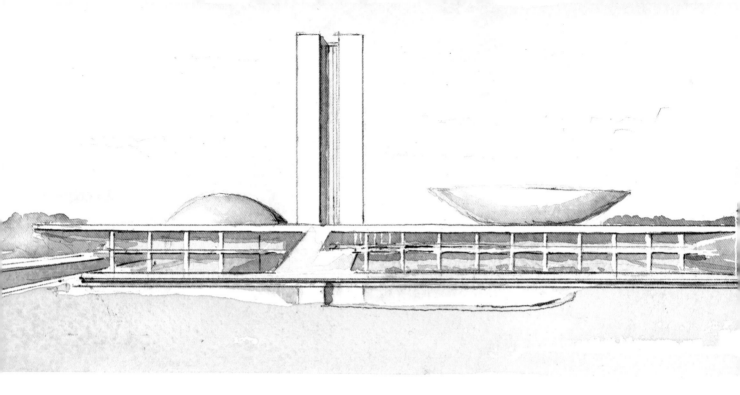

Plaza of the Three Powers, Brasilia 1958
Architect Oscar Niemeyer

President's Palace
Architect Oscar Niemeyer

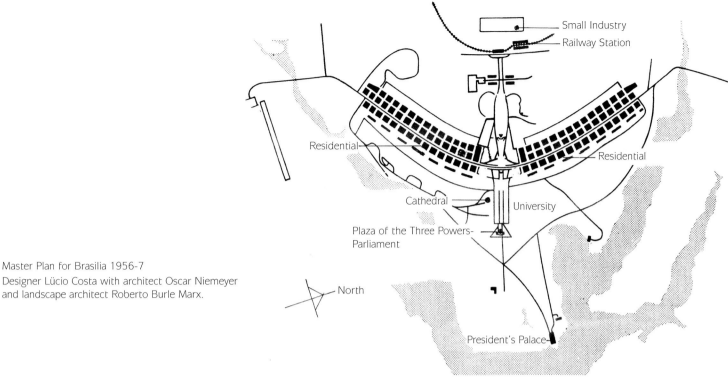

Master Plan for Brasilia 1956-7
Designer Lúcio Costa with architect Oscar Niemeyer
and landscape architect Roberto Burle Marx.

South America 1972

In 1972 the Concrete Society proposed a visit to South America and this attracted an enormous number of people –120 architects, builders, engineers and many others, to sign up to this trip.

We arrived in Argentina's Buenos Aires airport to discover that an important reception had been arranged for us to meet every one of importance in the city. It was a great time for contacts but the following day we were disappointed, as the tour company had no experience of showing or organizing visits to see interesting modern architecture.

We flew to Sao Paulo and again a reception was held on the first night, however the site visits afterwards did not improve. One of the temples on our itinerary was in a remote location in the jungle. The men's toilet facilities were a challenge to one very large member of the group who had been disabled by polio and was on crutches. The urinals were on the top of a flight of steps and there was no alternative but for him to perform from the bottom. A group of Japanese visitors came in at the time that our friend was relieving himself and thought that this was the customary practice!

Cathedral of Our Lady of Fatima Brasilia 1959-70
Architect Oscar Niemeyer

There was a free afternoon and as a friend of Bryan Organ who had made his first international sale of Malcolm Muggeridge's portrait to the Museum of Modern Art, I decided to go and see it hung and report back to Bryan. On my arrival at lunchtime I found that the museum was closed but would be open in the afternoon. There was a cafe where I decided to have lunch. I found it impossible to read the menu with my non-existent Portuguese and the waiter's lack of English. Someone on an adjoining table asked if they could help and the language problem was soon sorted out. They asked if I was enjoying South America. I explained the reason for our visit and said the major problem was that after our initial reception we were treated like ordinary tourists and were not being shown what we had expected to see. I told them that we were due to fly to Brasilia the next day and that I was concerned that the problem

Cathedral interior

would continue. One of the other members of the group who had been so helpful told me that he was an attorney with a bureau above the cafe in which we were having lunch. He said that Lucio Costa the designer of Brasilia was a close friend and he would see what he could do for us. After lunch he returned from his bureau and provided me with the telephone number of Lucio Costa. He told me that on arrival in Brasilia I should ring and he would come and meet with us to talk about his new city.

When I informed the other leading architects in the group, they could not understand how a young architect had managed to succeed in making contact with the designer of Brasilia. On arrival, we telephoned Lucio Costa who then came to meet us and we had a wonderful couple of hours with him. We discussed his work and he showed us his sketches of his buildings, which made our visit to Brasilia outstanding.

Hills of Rio de Janeiro

We then flew to Rio de Janeiro for a five-day visit. Rio is an unbelievably beautiful city but does have its dark side of slums and crime. At the airport a young student came and sat by me on the coach. He said that as we were such a large group the tour operators had enrolled a few students to come and help take us around. He asked me what I would like to see and I told him that the gardens of Roberto

Mosaic pavement along the Cocobana Beach by Roberto Burle MarX

Burle Marx were first on my list. With this he opened his case and produced the list of people who were to attend the reception for us the following day. Burle Marx was on it! He told me that he had met him and would introduce him to me at the reception. He then said he had a small car and offered to show us anything we liked for a small fee including the cost of petrol, which was a fantastic offer that we could not turn down.

Home of Roberto Burle Marx terrace decorated with the giant heads from the boats of the Amazon

Clive James, a couple of years earlier had made a program called 'A Postcard from Rio'. I had made a note of all the things he had experienced and thought this would be the basis for insuring that we did not miss anything of importance in this intriguing city. I decided that we should see the slums on the hills around Rio. It was quite an experience. We drove up to a point where we were close to a cafe and parked the car. He gathered together a group of children and told them that if the wheels were still on when we returned he would give them some money. He told us that it was not going to cost much. He took us to the bar where we met lots of interesting people. The Samba music was loud and we were invited to buy a drink for everyone. When we got back to the car the wheels were all intact and the children were paid, completing an interesting experience for us.

Roberto Burle Marx Estate and nursery near Rio de Janeiro run by his sister.
It is claimed the most important collection of tropical plants in the world.

Our next stop was the beach, which was full of beautiful females. The mountains made a perfect background.

In the evening he took us to a Voodoo ceremony, an experience that was not very enjoyable. It is a religious ritual of intense physical, emotional and spiritual out-pouring in public. Its aim is to try and establish contact with the ancestors and a higher being. We were pleased to get away after a reasonably short period of time.

Clive James in his program had visited a local hospital where he had witnessed women having adjustments to their breasts (boob jobs!) but we did not make this a feature of our itinerary!

At the reception my new young friend introduced me to Roberto Burle Marx. We had a long conversation and I asked him if it was possible to visit some of the gardens he had designed. He immediately said yes and suggested we first visited his estate and the nurseries to see the range of tropical plants.

His estate and nurseries were run by his sister and a team of gardeners. They had cultivated 3,500 species of plants for his landscape schemes. Roberto regularly visited the jungle, Savannah and the mountains of Brazil to bring back more plants. At an early age he discovered that in the tropics people

Cavanelas garden by Roberto Burle Marx house by Oscar Niemeyer

were trying to create European gardens but they found it impossible to keep the plants alive. He then changed to using native plants rather than European varieties. His unique designs and gardens became world famous. His work as a landscape architect and plant hunter resulted in one of the world's most important collections of tropical plants, at his home, Santa Antonio da Bica, just outside Rio.

For me, the most important features of Roberto Burle Marx's work were his skill as a manipulator of the landscape, re-contouring the ground to fit in with the design of the scheme and his deep empathy with plants. Roberto was not only a landscape architect but also a painter and treated gardens as works of art. He also took the opportunity to create timeless solutions and became famous

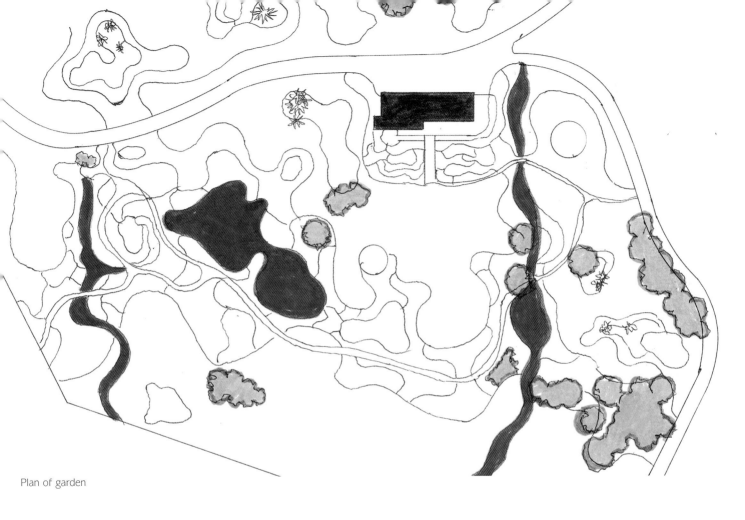

Plan of garden

at an early age for the roof garden of the Ministry of Education in Rio, designed by Le Corbusier. His aim was also to give the public a dignified way of living a balanced life with the major open spaces in Rio. He designed the huge bay front gardens in Rio, reclaiming a project linking the elegant quarters, airport and the city Centre including the two-mile mosaic pavement of black and white tiles in bold patterns along the Cocobana Beach.

The young man who was driving us around, took us to the nursery on the Marx estate and during our visit a message came from Roberto that we could go and look at two gardens high up above Rio. As soon as the news got around that we were organizing a coach to take those interested, it

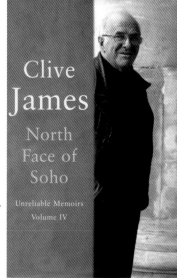

To Douglas —
Congpanes
Viva Rio!

Clive and Douglas – good memories of Rio in the the 1970s. Leicester 2008.

Shanty town or 'favela' slums on the hillsides of Rio de Janeiro

turned out that the whole company wanted to go. In the end four coaches went on this fantastic ride to look at the beautiful gardens high above Rio, created by this incredible man Roberto Burle Marx. We found the gardens lived up to his high standards. He had said, when designing groups of plants, you should never make a salad out of the garden but use bold inter-locking shapes or drifts of natural plants from the Amazon.

The garden was laid out in the midst of grazing country. It was a large garden designed to go with the large farm. A bold rhythmic composition with a great variety of plant groups contributed to its spacial quality. There was a strict control of colours and shapes and yet at the same time there were subtle surprises. For example a little waterfall, purposely half hidden, with a stream merging to babble through the garden.The composition of his naturalist landscape and use of natural plants links the garden with the grand landscape beyond. The space creates an anthology with the sumptuous landscape surrounding it. It was exciting to see these exquisite gardens by Roberto Burle Marx. We agreed his influence should continue, for all those interested in gardening in the tropics. It was a very memorable visit to South America.

Christ the Redeemer dominates the city

Rural China in 1984

China 1984 and 2009

In 1984 we made our first visit to China, when they started to open up the country to tourism. We flew British Airways to Moscow where we had a three-hour stop over. A fellow traveler who was an antiquarian bookseller would not admit to the Russian authorities that he had steel hips and was strip-searched as they were setting off the detection devices. After this excitement our journey continued with China Air but the aircraft had been at the airport without heating and it was very cold. The luggage compartments had no doors and as the aircraft ran down the runway the luggage descend onto our laps. The Director of 'Birdquest', the ornithological tour company was sitting close by and we discussed the plans for our visit. It was the first opportunity to discover more about China. He told me he was to lead a group of bird watchers in a few month's time to Tibet. He said he was going to hire

Great Wall of China from the Ming Dynasty.
The world's greatest mega-structure.

77

Beijing International biggest airport in the world
Architects Norman Foster and Partners
A very large building to a human scale

Too early to check in to hotel so off to Hutong old courtyard housing

Shanghai

a bicycle and I told him that my guide-book stated that it was not possible for visitors as all cycles were registered.

On our way to the hotel it was announced that we would be visiting 'The Great Wall'. It was a wonderful opportunity to see this impressive structure to remind us that the civilization of modern China stretches back more than 2,500 years. My ornithological friend discovered that if you take a taxi from the hotel and did not pay the fare on arrival, the driver would wait and bring you back and only charge for the return journey and not for the waiting time, hence he never needed to try to hire a bicycle. We returned from the fresh air of the country to discover Beijing dense in smog, which persisted day after day. The city was densely populated with mass housing packed together, in large neighborhoods with only footpath access. Piles of coke near the roads were used for fueling the single stove per dwelling for cooking and heating. The fumes hung over the city. These areas were in sharp contrast to the opulent palaces, temples, parks and gardens that covered the vast area of Beijing.

80

We returned to China in 2009 for a five star special credit-crunch offer by China Travel, through Voyages Jules Verne, to find an unrecognizable change. We arrived at a beautiful airport, the largest in the world, the scale of which was superbly handled by the designer Norman Foster and Partners. The city with new housing and roads reflected China's desire to make an impact on the world for the 2008 Summer Olympics. We had a brief visit to the National Stadium, nicknamed the 'bird's nest'. This is the world's largest steel structure designed by Herzog and de Menron with Arup Sport, China's Architectural Design Research Group. The structural engineers were Arup.

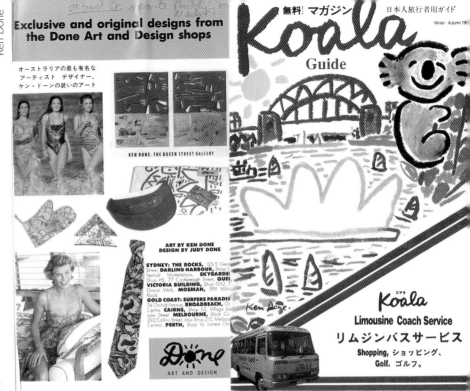

Artist Ken Done using the images of Sydney

Sydney Australia 1991 and 2008

The Sydney Opera House was on our radar since its completion in 1967. With family to visit in Melbourne, we took the opportunity to visit many parts of this vast continent, over many years, visiting Sydney to study the Opera House several times. Jørn Utzon won the competition with the brilliant design of the soaring white curves of the shells, each slightly different, unlike the simpler shells of Nervi of Italy and Felix Candela of Mexico and Spain. The shell designs of the Opera House, in Sydney, were especially difficult and Arup, one of the great international structural engineering, companies could not solve the structural problem of the dynamic forms despite the use of four main-frame

ydney Opera House from the air. Architect Jørn Utzon

The Bennelong Restaurant provides the
best view of the interior of the roof.
Sketches¬ during dinner

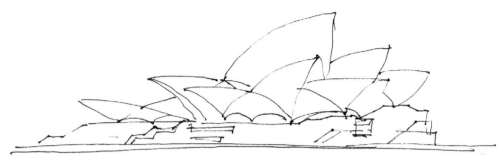

Sketch of Utzon's competition entry
The poetic conceptual and visionary gift

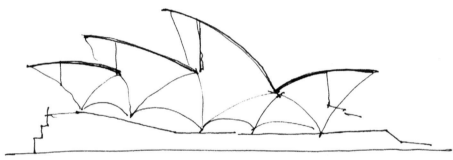

Sketch of single skin reinforced concrete shell from the competition drawings of 1957

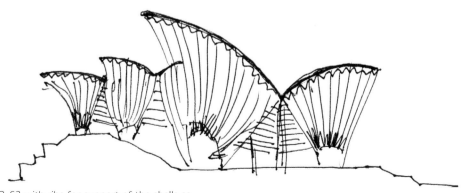

Sketch of the final drawings 1962-63 with ribs for support of the shells as
neither man nor computers in those days could prove the shell design safe.

A magical day 30.01.2008
Waking to see from the hotel bedroom the building in sun light
Morning harbour cruise
Afternoon helicopter flight to see this world famous building in its setting.
Evening dinner in the Bennelong Restaurant
We remembered the words of Jørn Utzon who wrote in 1948 'At the same time the architect must have the ability to imagine and to create, an ability that is sometimes called fantasy, sometimes dream.'

ydney Opera House from the water.
. M. The Queen opened it in 1973

computers. Costs spiralled out of control and Utzon resigned. The structural problem was solved by supporting the shells with ribs that visually affected the elegance of the structures from the inside and is unfortunately disappointing. However the exterior is magnificent, the shells sparkle with the sun lit reflections of the surrounding water. It is one of the great sights of the world with the sails in the harbour echoing the silhouette of the bridge and a striking icon for Australia.

Picasso
Le Guitariste (The Guitarist), 1910

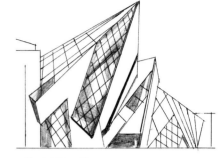

Le Corbusier

Daniel Libeskin

Kandinsky
Yellow-Red-Blue, 1925

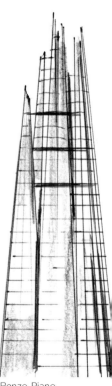

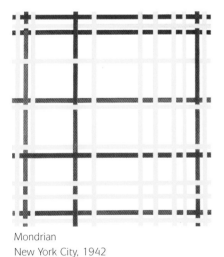

Mondrian
New York City, 1942

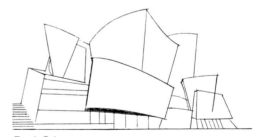

Frank Gehry

Renzo Piano

The new architecture is anti-cubic; that is, it does not seek to fix the vatious space cells together with a closed cube, but draws the functional space cells… away from the centre… towards the outside, wherebt height, width, depth + time tend towards a wholly new plastic expression in open space. In this way architecture acquires a more or less floating aspect, that as it were, works against the gravitational forces of nature.
Theo van Doesburg, 1924

Legacy of art and buildings of the Modern Movement

Picasso's genius is beyond doubt. He was an explorer of space, an inventor of techniques, and a creator of forms. Picasso truly created a revolution in art by questioning age old techniques of pictorial space and form. The impact of his work was widespread reaching not just other artists but composers, authors, and architects of the twentieth century.
  James Joyce

It is possible to start the Modern Period with the Arts and Craft Movement in Britain but this book commenced with the Crystal Palace. The changing world has challenged the architects to respond with what have been labeled 'Expressionism', 'Constructivism' and the 'International Style'. Traditional and new materials have given architects a freedom to produce exciting buildings to satisfy the brief and a dramatic change of scale of many buildings.

The impact of Cubism was immense spreading across the world not only in art but also architecture.

Art and architecture were responding to cubism, spacial concepts and space time ideas. Picasso and Le Corbusier and many involved with the Bauhaus including Wassily Kandinsky first in Germany and then spreading across Europe to America were prime movers.

It is impossible to include all the great buildings and architects of the Modern Movement. My choice is the following my travels around the world.

Frank Lloyd Wright

The mother art is architecture.
Without an architecture of our own we
have no soul of our own civilization.
 Frank Lloyd Wright

Robie House 1910 Chicago

Frank Lloyd Wright made a significant impact first in America and then in the rest of the world, including the Far East. The Prairie House, which was influenced by Wright's interest in the house and garden design of Japan and helped to change the design of domestic architecture. The Johnson Wax Building, Racine, Wisconsin made those designing industrial and commercial buildings think again. Fallingwater, Pennsylvania, 1935-37 fused in a brilliant way the building and landscape completely.

Cooney House 1908 Illinois

Fallingwater, Bear Run 1935 Pennsylvania

Le Corbusier

Space and light and order.
Those are the things that
men need just as much as
they need bread or a place to sleep.
  Le Corbusier

Le Corbusier, described by many as the founder of Modern Architecture, through his buildings, writings and the ideas for proportions 'The Modula' an harmonious measure to the human scale universally applicable to architecture and mechanics. Halls of Residencies in the world changed when the design of 'Maison Suisse' was built in Paris in 1930-32. Domestic architecture was influenced by his Villa Savoy, Poissy, and later Masons Jaoul in Paris. Le Corbusier's ideas spread through Europe, America and the Far East. Oscar Niemeyer was a great exponent in South America. Unité d' Habitation in Marseilles put into practice his theory for dwellings in a landscape park as the alternative to the slums of mass housing. In India the city of Chandigarth gave Le Corbusier an opportunity to put many of his ideas into practice for a whole city. For me the remarkable and beautiful Chapel of Notre Dame-du-Haut at Ronchamp 1950-54 is exceptional.

Chapel Notre-Dame du Haut, Ronchamp 1955
Jonathan Glancy on the debt Le Corbusier owes to Picasso 'The Chapel at Ronchamp is one of the world's great works of art: it happens to be a building, yet one that is far more than simply a roof over bowed heads.'

Plan
Designed to provide peace and silence inside and a focal point for the Pilgrims outside with the altar and pulpit for both.

93

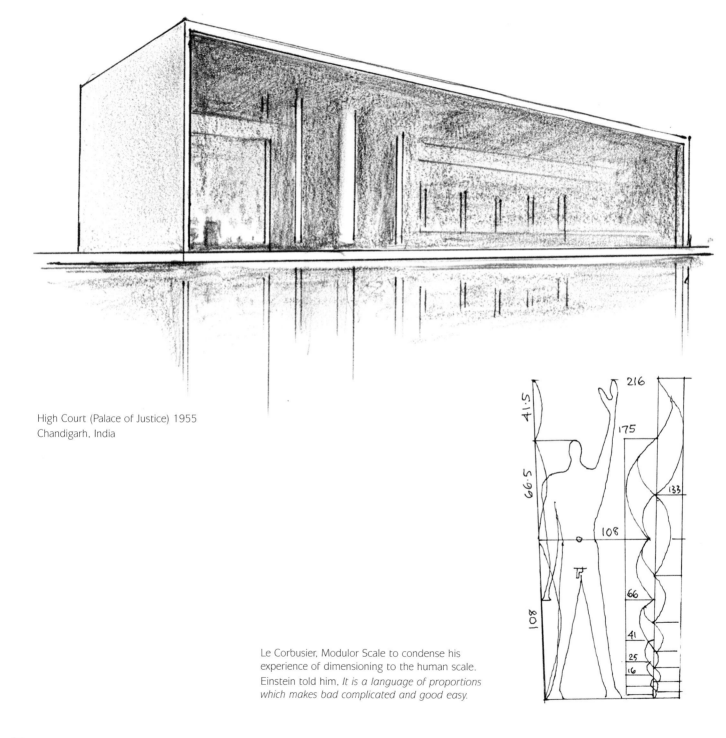

High Court (Palace of Justice) 1955
Chandigarh, India

41.5

66.5

108

216

175

133

108

66

41

25

16

Le Corbusier, Modulor Scale to condense his
experience of dimensioning to the human scale.
Einstein told him, *It is a language of proportions
which makes bad complicated and good easy.*

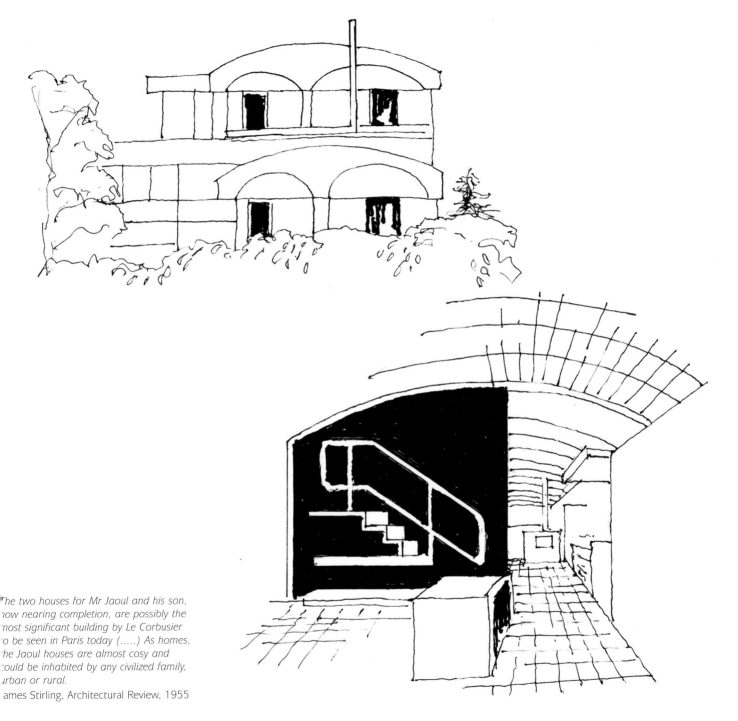

*The two houses for Mr Jaoul and his son,
now nearing completion, are possibly the
most significant building by Le Corbusier
to be seen in Paris today (.....) As homes,
the Jaoul houses are almost cosy and
could be inhabited by any civilized family,
urban or rural.*
James Stirling, Architectural Review, 1955

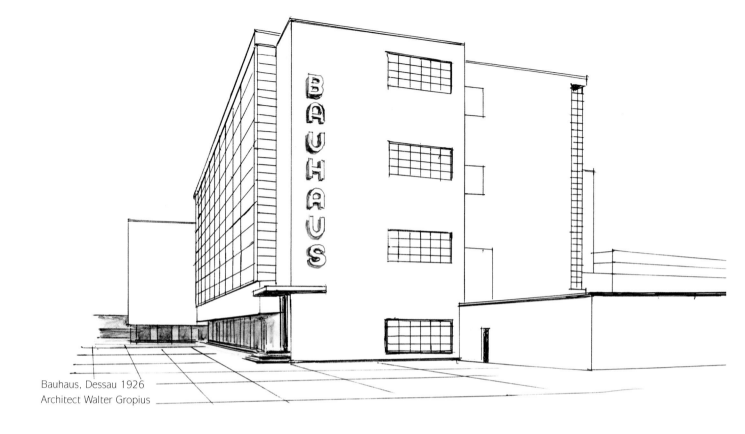

Bauhaus, Dessau 1926
Architect Walter Gropius

Walter Gropius and Mies van der Rohe

Architecture begins where engineering ends.
Walter Gropius

The Bauhaus was an art school founded by Walter Gropius in Germany which later moved to America. It had a profound influence on art, architecture, graphic design, interior design, industrial design and typography. The work of Mies van der Rohe changed the world with his designs for large and small buildings constructed in steel and glass. A superb and beautiful example is the Barcelona German Pavilion for the 1929 Exhibition, taken down after the exhibition and more recently rebuilt faithfully to the original design. It is still a modern masterpiece of design and proportion together with the 'Barcelona Chair' designed for the same exhibition. These have become classic design icons of today.

...erman Pavilion, 1929, Barcelona
...rchitect Mies van der Rohe. who said:
...rchitecture starts when you carefully put two bricks together.
...here it begins.

Barcelona chair 1929

Architect Mies van der Rohe

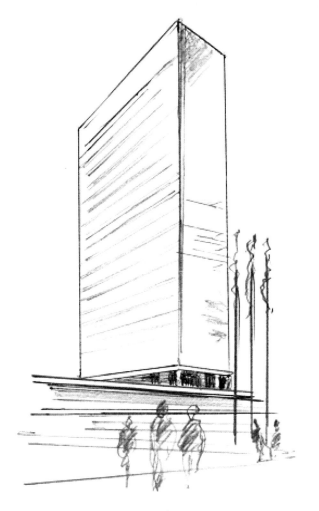

Seagram Building New York 1954

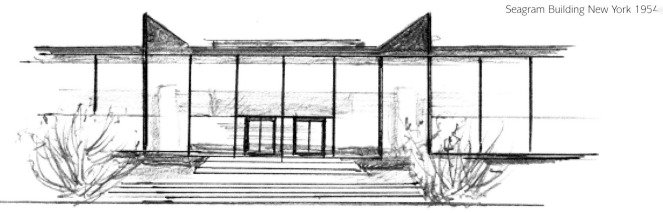

Illinois Institute of Technology, Chica

Faculty of Engineering, University of Leicester 1963
Architects James Stirling & James Gowan

Neue Staasgallerie, Stuttgart 1977-84
Architects James Stirling, Michael Wilford Associates

James Stirling

James Stirling was to break the mould of classical building designs for universities when he designed the 'Engineering Building' at the University of Leicester 1959-63. He was influenced by Pavilion Suisse by Le Corbusier. At Leicester the individual elements of laboratories, administration tower, lecture theaters and circulation were clearly expressed in a bold composition. The functional use of each element was not compromised by the architecture. The idea spread rapidly and many architects came to study the building from America and Japan. Stirling followed this building with the History Faculty Building, at Cambridge, then 'Queen's College, Oxford and Neue Staasgalerie, Stuttgart 1977-84.

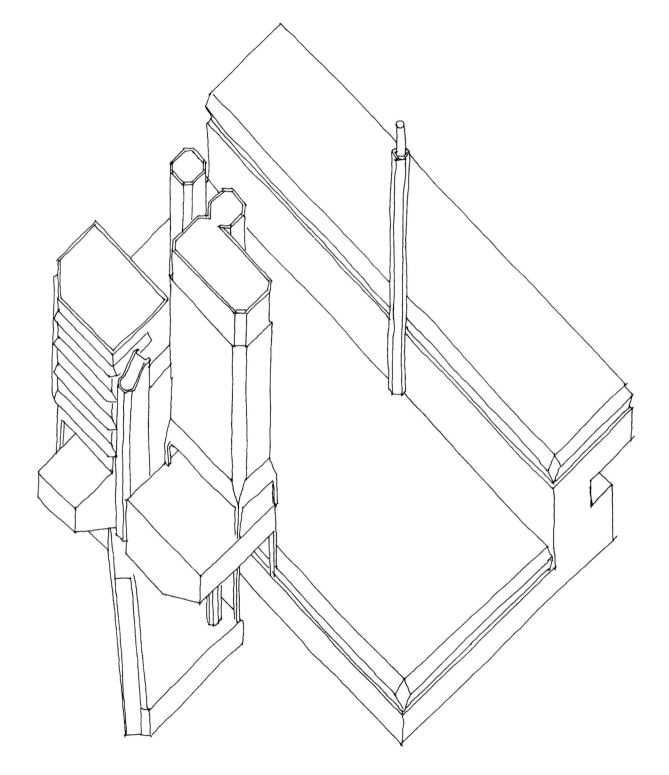

Faculty of Engineering, University of Leicester 1963
Architects James Stirling & James Gowan

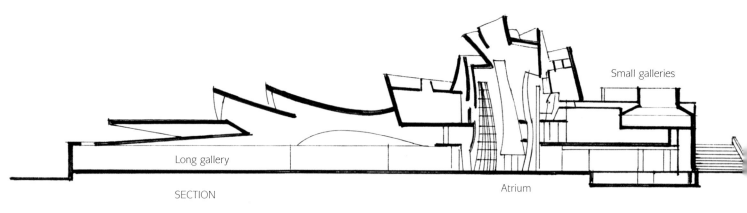

Long gallery

SECTION

Small galleries

Atrium

Guggenheim Museum Bilbao, Spain by Frank Gehry
The design inspired by Picasso's cubist painting 'The Accordionist',
was only made possible by the innovative use of computer-aided
design tools created for the aerospace industry.

Frank Gehry

Architecture should speak of its time and place,
but yearns for timelessness.
   Frank Gehry.
   Gehry says he has always wanted an architecture
   that looks like work in progress and has movement to it.

Frank Gehry surprised many with his design of the Guggenheim Museum, Bilbao, Spain 1997. Philip Johnson said that 'it was the greatest building of our time'. Philip Jodiolio said 'moored to the banks of the River Nervion, the great titanium flagship is not only one of the symbols of Bilbao's regeneration, but also one of the American architect's most spectacular works'. The flowing shapes of Gehry's buildings make them immediately recognizable any were in the world.

Atrium inspired by the flowing
line of dance of Fred Astaire
and Ginger Rogers. Gehry likes
movement in his buildings.

Dancing House Prague 1992-96
Architects Frank Gehry and Croatian-Czech architect Vlado Miluni

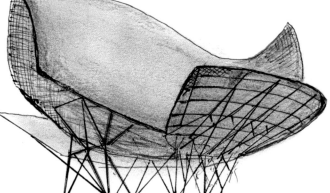

Fish sculpture for the 1992 Barcelona Olympics

Walt Disney Concert Hall 2003

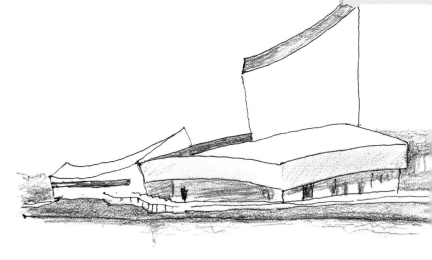

Daniel Libeskin

To provide meaningful architecture
is not to parody history but to articulate it.
  Daniel Libeskin

Daniel Libeskin came to the attention of the world with the design of the Jewish Museum, in Berlin and his work can be seen in the Royal Ontario Museum, Canada and The Imperial War Museum North in the UK. The architecture of Daniel Libeskin reflects his interest and involvement in philosophy, art, music, literature, theatre and film.

Jewish Museum Berlin

Royal Ontario Museum Canada

The Brits Who Built
the Modern World

Carré D'Art and reflecting the Roman Maison Carrée, Nimes.

Norman Foster

*As an architect you design for the present,
with an awareness of the past, for a future
which is essentially unknown.*
  Norman Foster

British architects, more than most, have responded to the changing needs of the 20th and 21st Century and have an almost unrivaled reputation around the world for daring, innovation, creativity and flair. This is demonstrated in the 2014 BBC 4 television series, 'The Brits Who Built the Modern World, 1950-2012'. Norman Foster had been a great exponent, first with the Hong Kong Bank, the Sainsbury Centre for Visual Arts, The University of East Anglia 1978. In 1999 he won the competition for the design of the New German Parliament Reichstag building in Berlin. This was an innovative design with spiraled ramps providing the means of moving through the structure. Foster and Partners are adept at handling scale creating large but unthreatening buildings for the user. They enjoy the varied challenge of the design of airports, bridges and other engineering projects. The Millau Viaduct 2004, is the largest bridge in the world, spanning the River Tarn in southern France. The deck of the bridge is further from the valley below than the height of the Eiffel Tower. At times clouds float below the road.

Sainsbury Centre Norwich with sculpture
Female Form by Henry Moore

109

Reichstag New German Parliament Berlin 1999

Millau Viaduct, central France

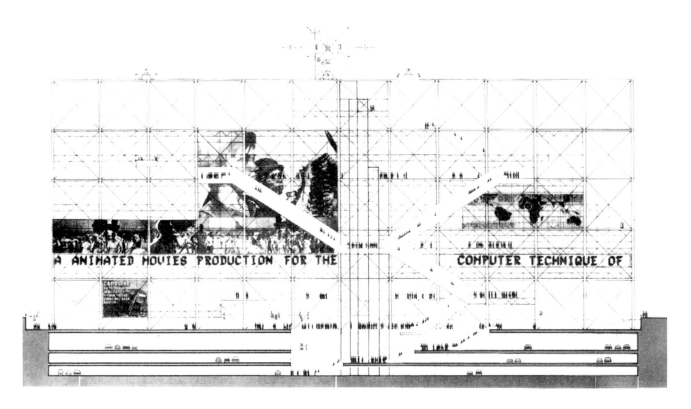

Sketch of the Competition drawing for the Centre Pompidou
by architects Piano & Roger

Renzo Piano, Su and Richard Rogers

*The only way forward, if we are going to improve the
quality of the environment, is to get everybody involved.*
  Richard Rogers

Renzo Piano, Su and Richard Rogers designed the Pompidou Centre, 1977 which looked like nothing
that had been built before. It was designed with all of the services, which need replacing frequently,
positioned on the outside of the building, leaving large clear open spaces inside. Rogers and Partners
continued with the Lloyd's Building, Millennium Dome, Madrid Airport and many more.

Waterloo Station Architect Nicholas Grimshaw
Eurostar trains designed by the Italian design
house Pininfarina and Trelleborg Industrial AVS
of Leicester were involved with its Metalastik
branded design.

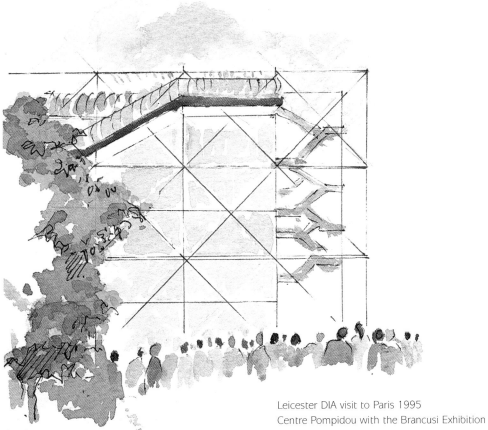

Leicester DIA visit to Paris 1995
Centre Pompidou with the Brancusi Exhibition

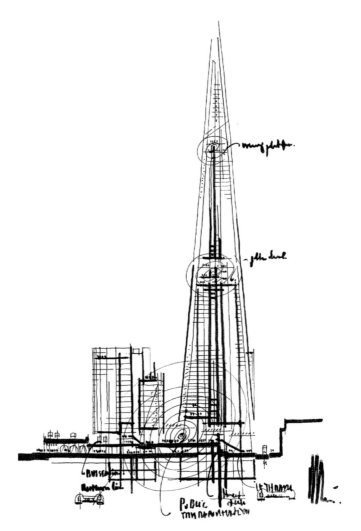

Renzo Piano

*One of the great beauties of architecture is that
each time, it is like life starting all over again.*
   Renzo Piano

Copy of sketch by Renzo Piano of the Shard

Renzo Piano designed The Shard, 2009. It is superb and the tallest building in Western Europe. Built above London Bridge Station, with viewing galleries on floors 68 to 72, offices 2 - 28, the restaurant floors 31-33, a hotel 34-52, residencies 53-65 and floor 78 is reserved for functions for the super-rich.
   There were many more listed in the BBC and RIBA Publication 'The Brits who Built the Modern World'.

hard with Tower Bridge at sunset

London Aquatic Centre for the 2012 Olympic Games
Architects Zaha Hadid

Conclusion

There are 360 degrees, so why stick to one?
  Zaha Hadid

It is fascinating to speculate what the future will be for new Architectural design. Zaha Hadid, the Iraqi - British architect is producing exciting designs around the world incorporating free flowing forms and rarely, if ever, a right angle. Innovative design has been freed by the computers capabilities, new materials and even, perhaps, three-dimensional scanning. Zaha Hadid's designs are daring and visionary. Examples can be seen at the Aquatic Centre, Olympic Park London, the new Serpentine Gallery Restaurant and further afield the Heydar Aliyev Centre Azerbaijan, 2013.

Magazine Restaurant, Serpentine Galleries London 2013
Architects Zaha Hadid

Heydar Aliyev Centre, Baku, Azerbaijan 2013
Architects Zaha Hadid